Slap & Pop Technique for Guitar

by Jean Marc Belkadi

MUSICIANS INSTITUTE
PRIVATE LESSONS

ISBN 0-634-03210-0

HAL•LEONARD CORPORATION

7777 W. BLUEMOUND RD. P.O. BOX 13819 MILWAUKEE, WI 53213

Copyright © 2001 by HAL LEONARD CORPORATION
International Copyright Secured   All Rights Reserved

No part of this publication may be reproduced in any form or by any means without the prior written permission of the Publisher.

Visit Hal Leonard Online at
www.halleonard.com

Table of Contents

Page		CD Tracks
4	Introduction	
5	Technical Performance Notes	
5	About the Audio	
6	Chapter 1: Funk Figures	1–20
13	Chapter 2: Funk-Rock Figures	21–26
15	Chapter 3: R&B and Motown Figures	27–30
17	Chapter 4: Latin and Reggae Figures	31–34
18	Chapter 5: Technical Exercises	35–52
23	Acknowledgments	
23	About the Author	

Note: Use Track 53 to tune up.

Introduction

The purpose of this book is to provide a fresh perspective on the subject of funk guitar. For years, I played funk the way most guitarist do—with a pick. This sound is certainly a staple of funk music and a must-learn for all serious funk guitarists. After becoming increasingly interested in funk bass players and the techniques they used, however, I began experimenting with slap and pop techniques (commonly used with bass) in my guitar playing. Influenced by players such as Louis Johnson, Yanic Top, Marcus Miller, Stanley Clarke, Victor Wooten, and Kevin Eubanks, I began imitating the sounds I heard from them on my guitar. Years later, I've found that, although funk is an obvious choice, this technique can be applied to *many* styles. Throughout this book, we'll also see it applied to R&B, Motown, Reggae, and Latin styles. We'll also cover odd meters and straight-ahead funk-rock grooves. When it's all done, you'll have a new vocabulary of techniques to incorporate into your own playing.

Technical Performance Notes

In order to best digest the information in this book, it's probably necessary to discuss a few techniques that aren't commonly found in guitar notation. Below is a list of abbreviations and explanations that pertain to the musical figures found in this book. You may recognize many of these from conventional bass notation.

T – Strike or "slap" the string with the right-hand thumb.
P – Snap or "pop" the string by pulling upwards with the index finger of your right hand and quickly releasing it.
L – Slap the strings on the fretboard with your left-hand fingers laid flat, creating a muted percussive effect.
I – Strum with your right-hand index finger (downstroke) as if it were a pick.
⊕ – Hammer or "tap" the fret indicated with one of the fret-hand fingers.
F – Strum with the nail of your right-hand thumb (upstroke).

Though the "slap" technique is very familiar to most bass players, guitar players have usually not experimented with this before. Try different positions along the string to ensure that you are not producing a harmonic with your slap. Also, try to keep your right arm parallel to the strings.

About the Audio

Throughout this book, the numbers in the audio symbols (◆) indicate the CD track number where each figure will be found on the accompanying CD.

Chapter 1

Funk Figures

Though this technique can be applied to other styles (as we'll discover throughout this book), its most obvious use lies in the funk genre. Here are plenty of grooves to get you acclimated to this new technique.

These first two figures make use of the open E string, as this provides a great way to learn the slap-and-pop technique.

Fig. 1

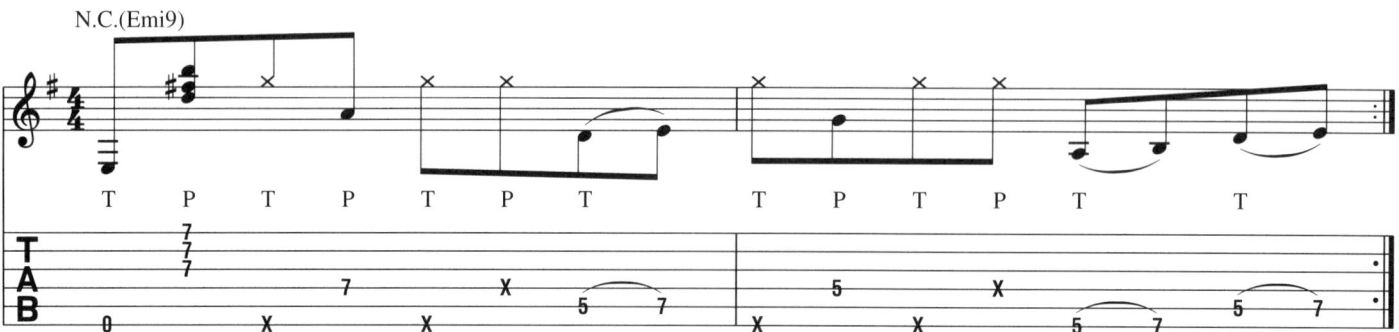

Fig. 2

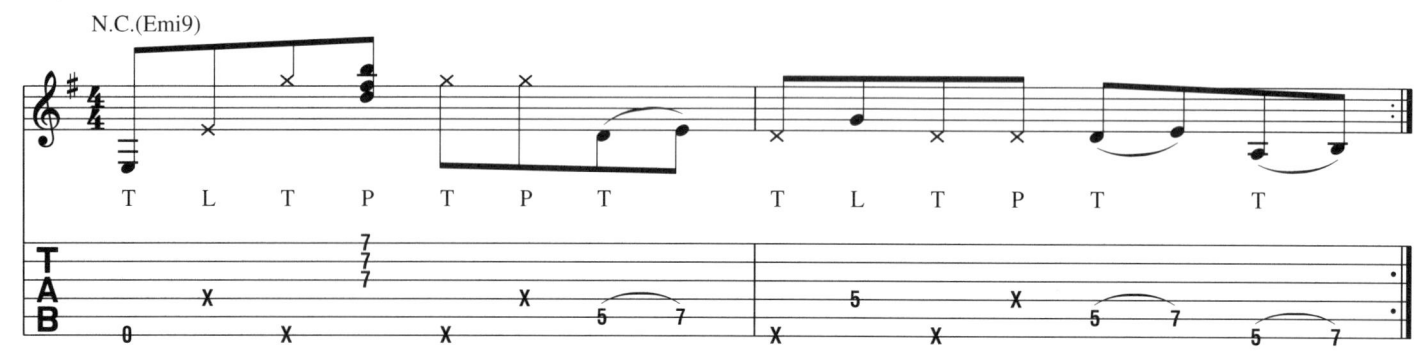

Figures 3 and 4 make use of slapping the A string. You'll probably find this a bit more difficult than the low E string, but with practice you'll be able to slap the fourth, fifth, and sixth strings all equally. Figure 3 uses a downstroke with the index finger to play the sliding double stop.

Fig. 3

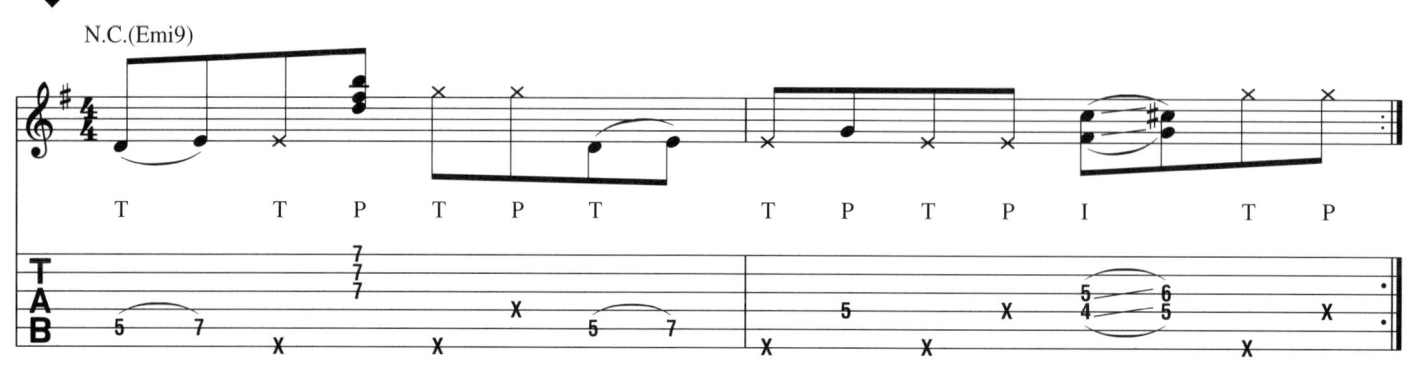

Fig. 4

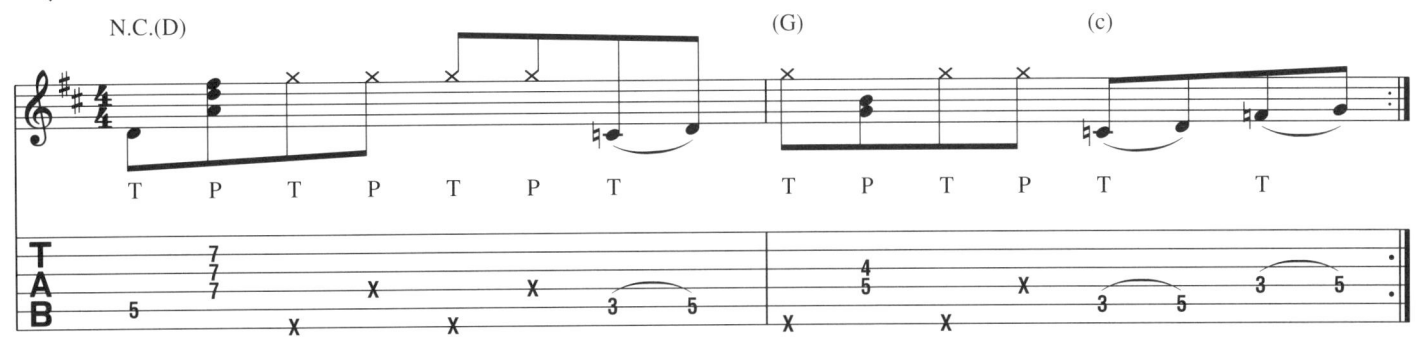

This figure introduces the left-hand muted slap technique. One of the key elements of this style is to keep the rhythm solid. This sometimes requires the use of the left hand to produce an occasional sixteenth-note percussive click.

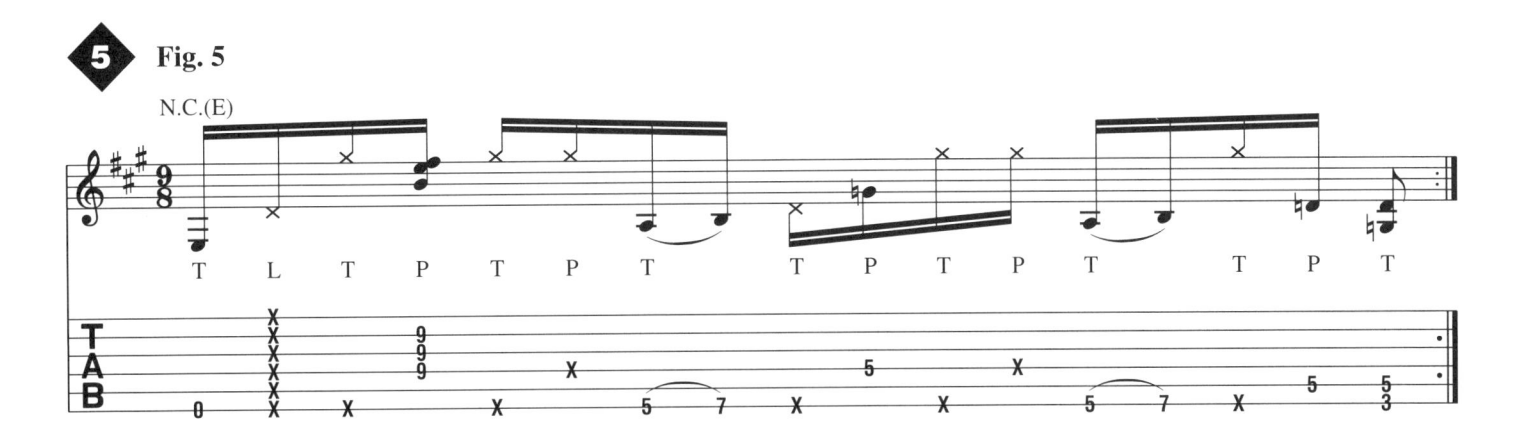

Fig. 5

Pay attention to the rhythm of the first beat in this next figure. This triplet hammer-on is a nice way to spice up an otherwise straight sixteenth-note riff. Notice also the index-finger downstroke on the F/G on beat 4.

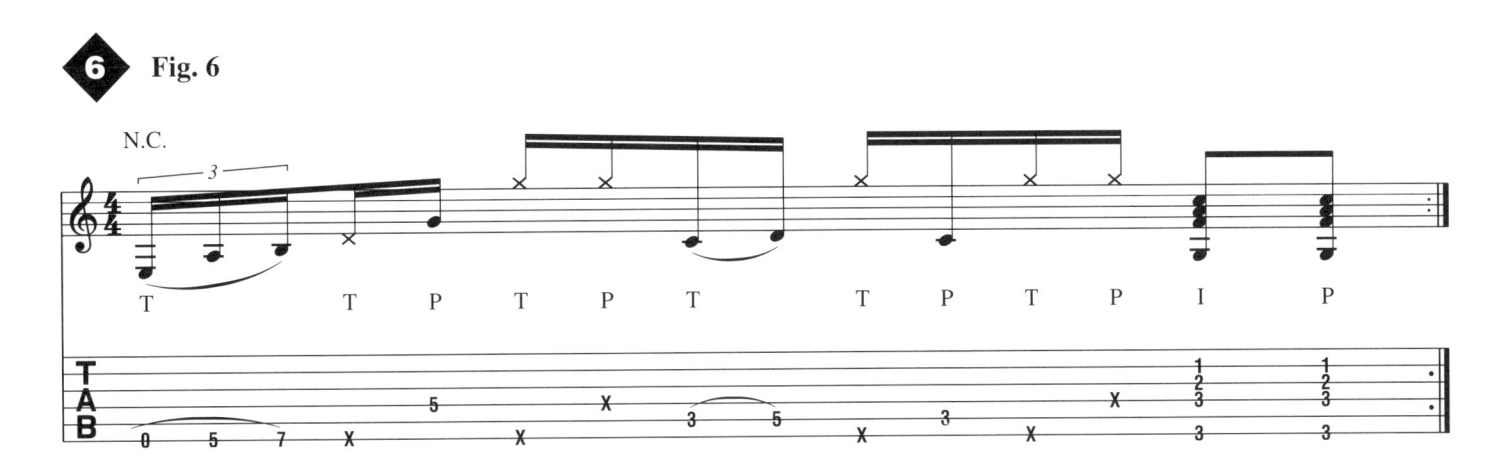

Fig. 6

Figures 7, 8, and 9 introduce the left-hand hammer-on technique. While figure 7 concentrates on the fifth and third strings, figures 8 and 9 concentrate on the sixth and fourth strings.

Fig. 7

Fig. 8

Fig. 9

This figure features a bluesy A Mixolydian sound and a chromatic sliding double stop. Try this one at both medium and fast tempos.

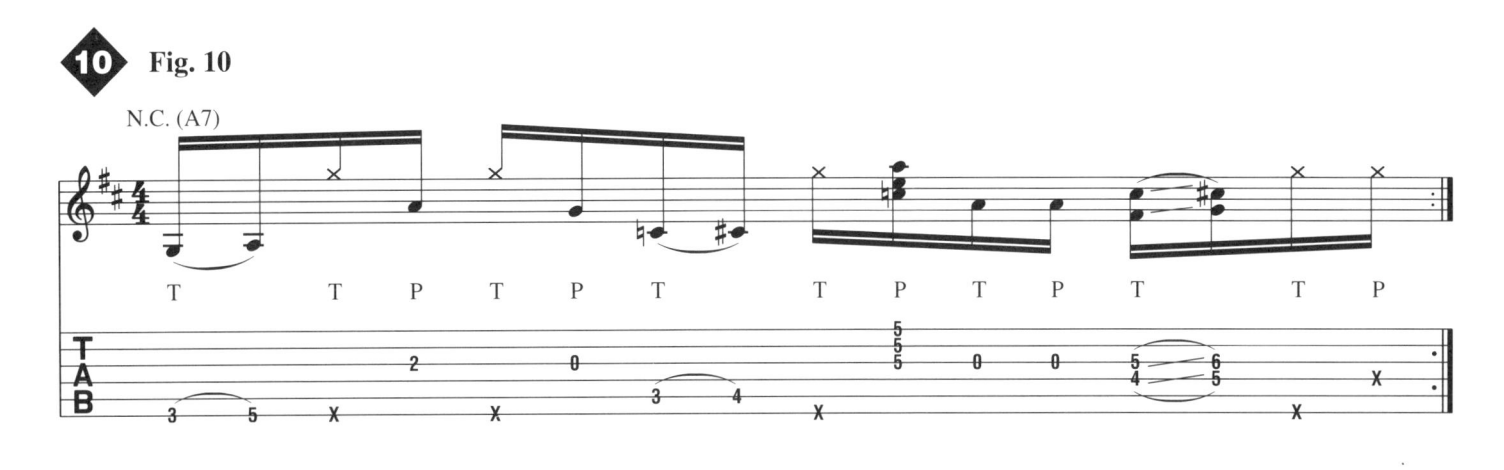

Fig. 10

Fig. 11 mixes triad punctuations with single-note riffing. Notice the implied A, C#mi, and D tonalities in measure 2.

Fig. 11

This figure in G minor features a disco-sounding progression, a serious groove, and a chromatic leading tone in beat 4 of measure 2.

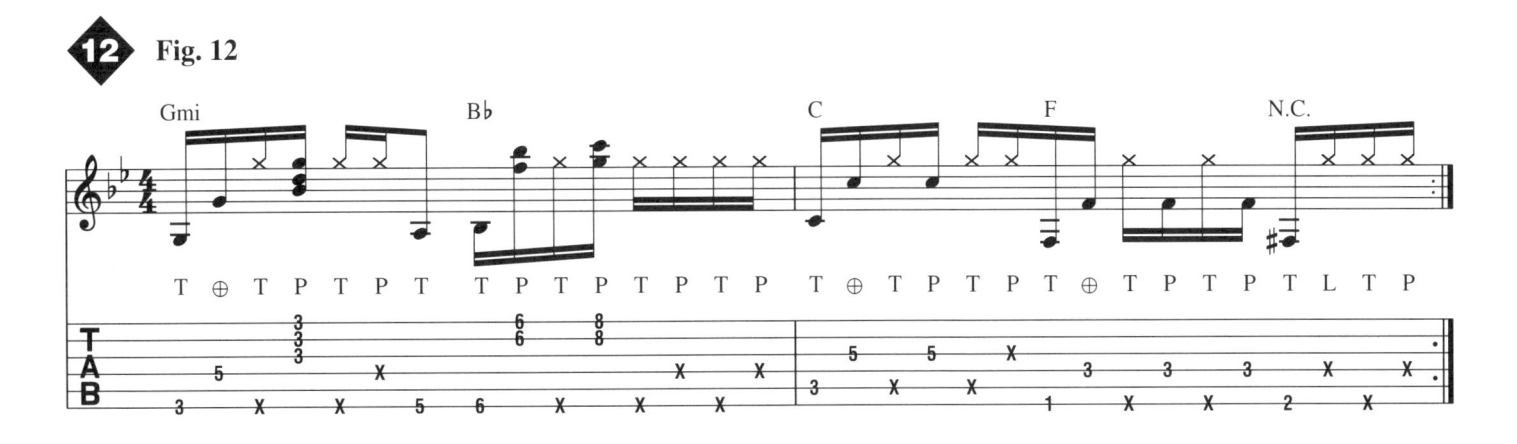

Fig. 12

The syncopation in this figure propels it forward with anticipation. Notice the chromatic chord movement in measure 2, leading nicely back to the F chord at the repeat.

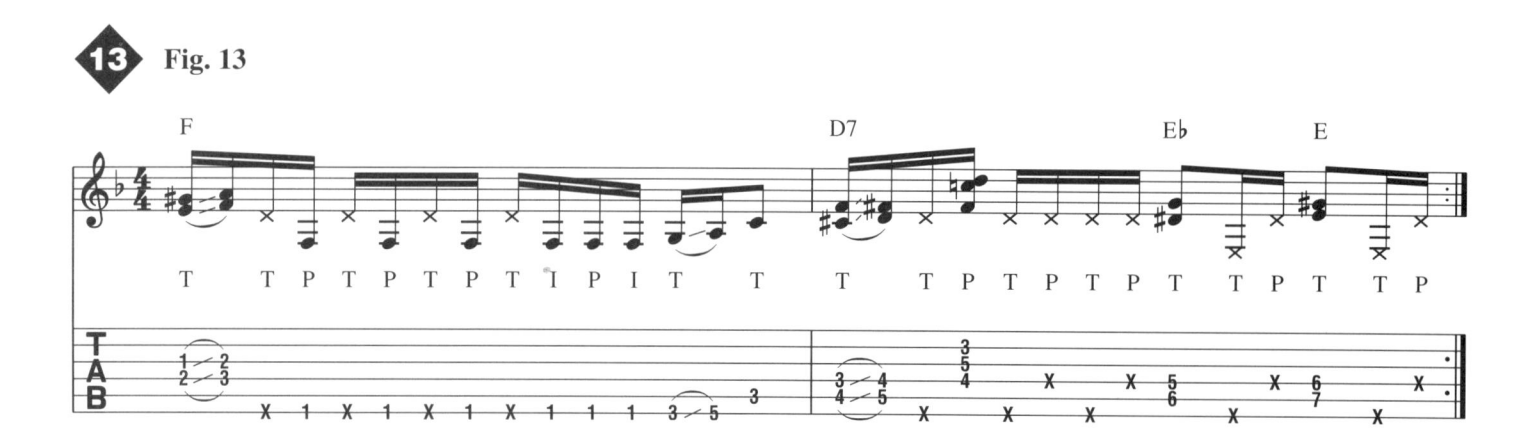

Fig. 13

This riff in C features sliding chromatic triple stops, syncopated chord punches, and a bluesy E♭–to–E hammer-on.

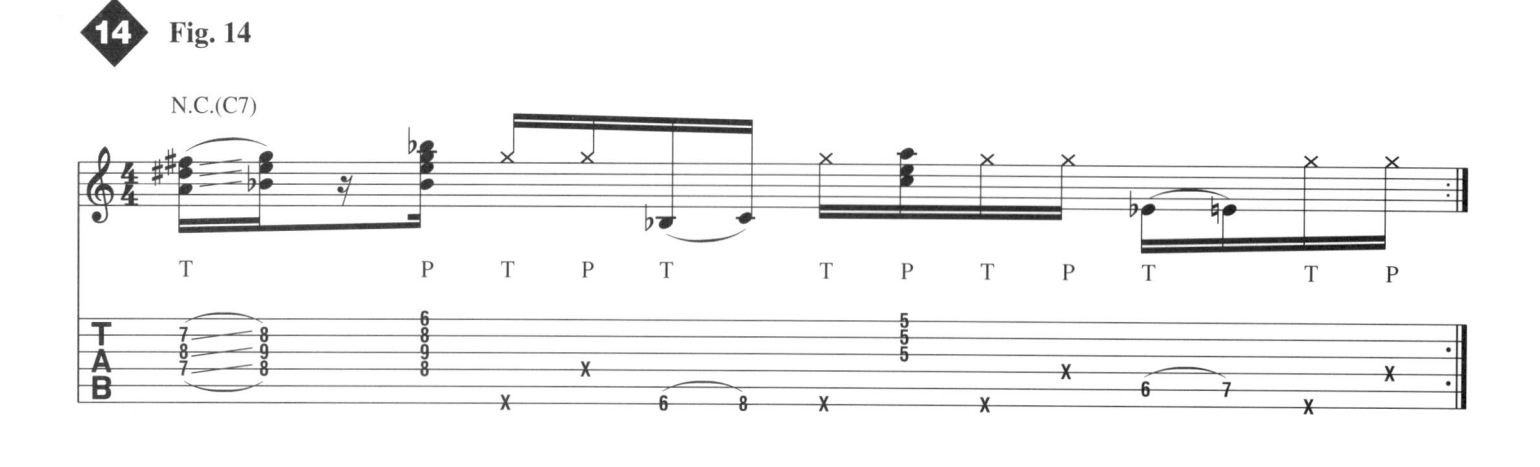

Fig. 14

Fig. 15 makes good use of accented chromatic approach notes in beats 1 and 4 of measure 2. Notice again the abundance of syncopated chord punches.

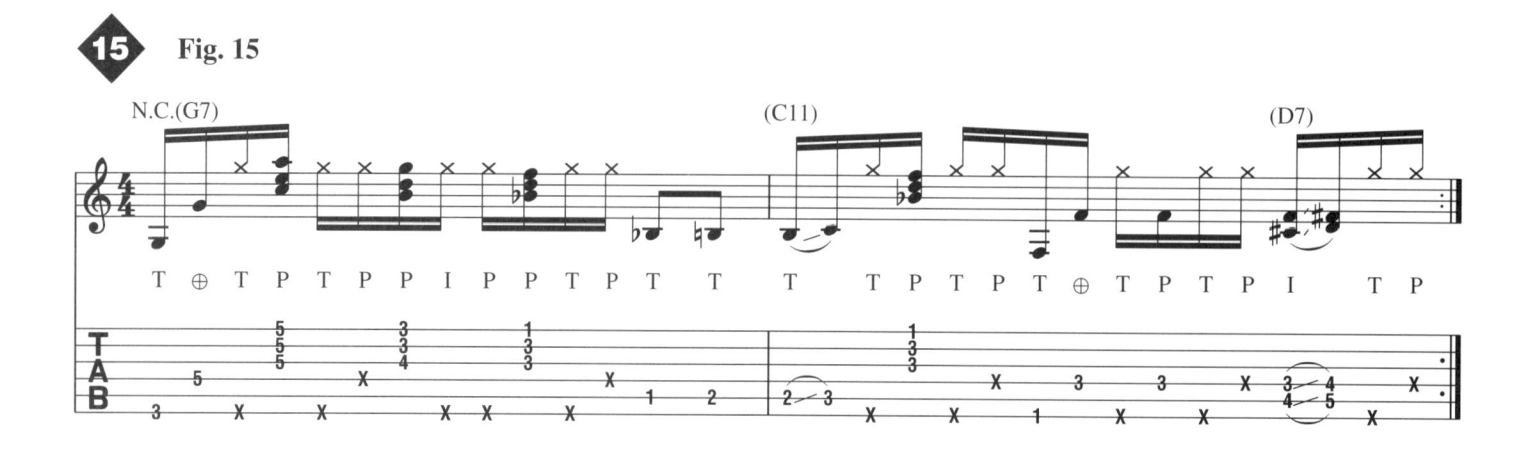

Fig. 15

The following two figures demonstrate bass-line figures played exclusively on the bottom three strings. A solid rhythmic feel is imperative in making these lines groove.

Fig. 16

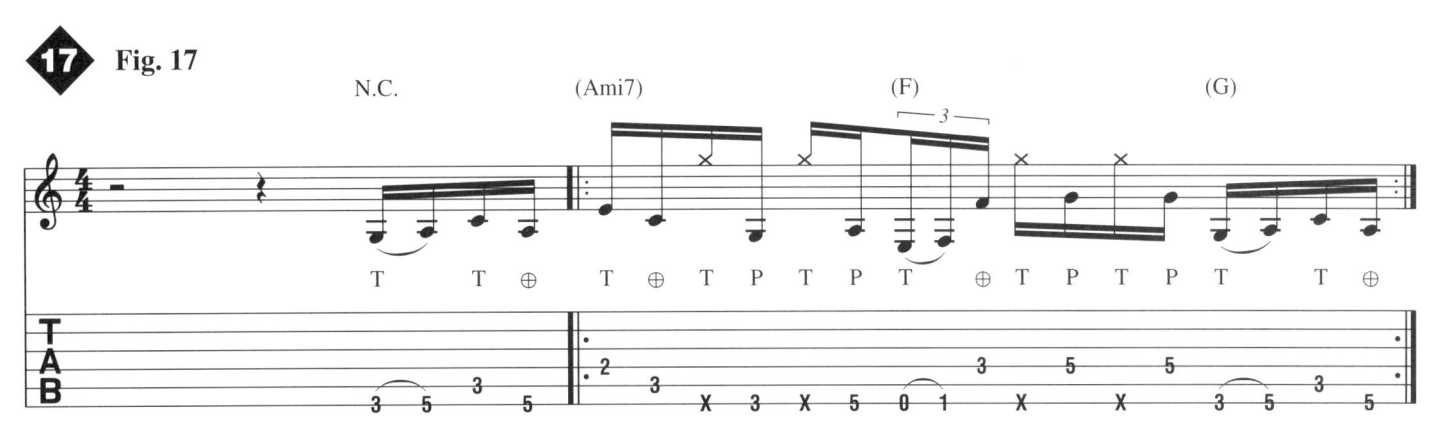

Fig. 17

This figure features right-hand tapping and index-finger strumming. Notice the bluesy hammer-on in measure 2, beat 2.

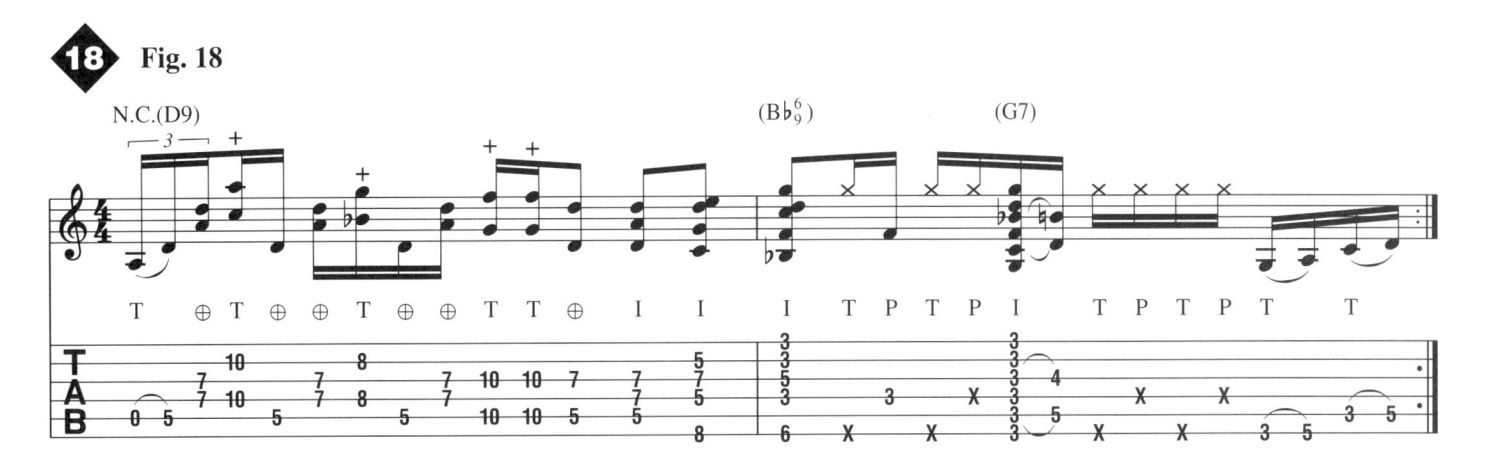

Fig. 18

11

This figure makes extensive use of the index-finger strumming technique. All of the chords belong to the key of F major, with the exception of the D major in beat 2 of measure 4. Notice that this chord is the only different element when the progression is repeated.

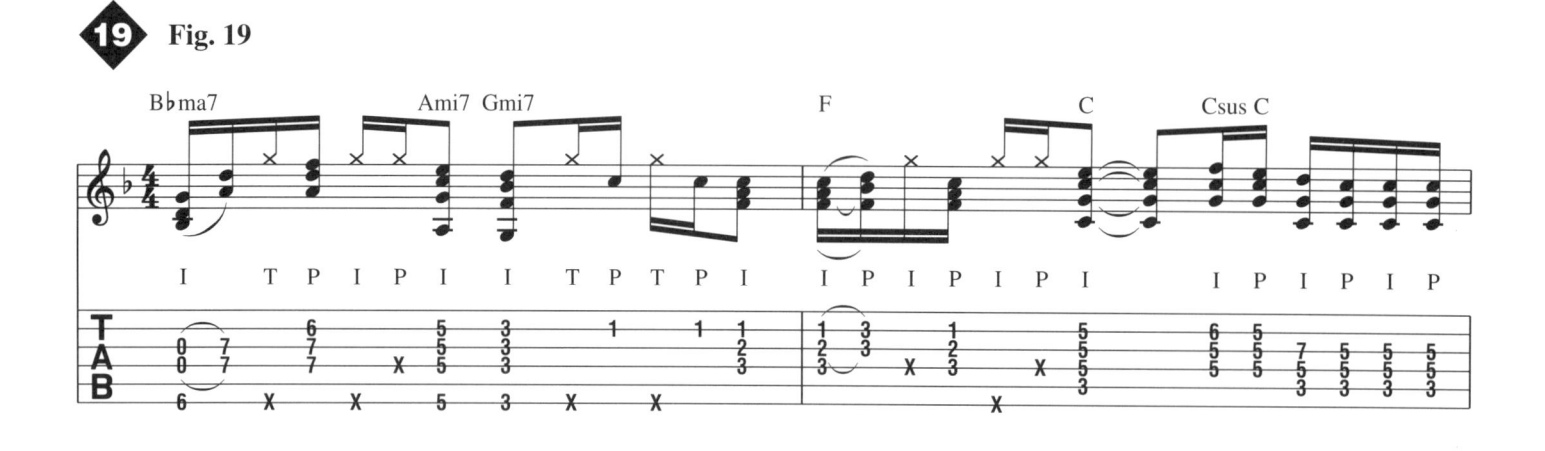

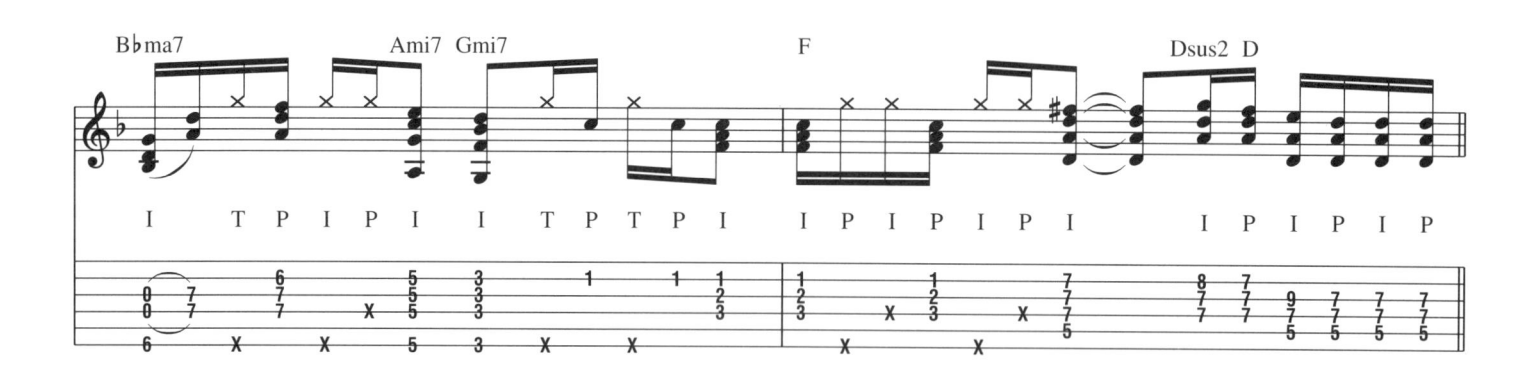

Fig. 19

Fig. 20, in E minor, features an effective combination of bass-note riffing (measure 1) and chordal strumming (measure 2). This two-measure vamp (Emi–C6/9) provides an excellent backdrop over which to improvise.

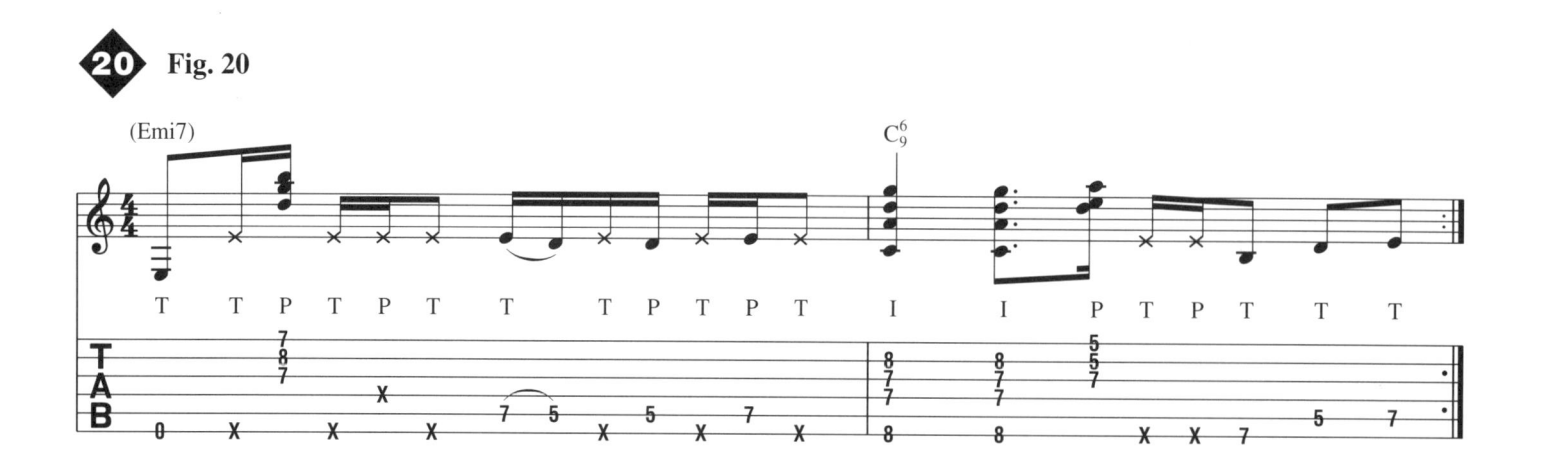

Fig. 20

Chapter 2

Funk-Rock Figures

This section provides a few "four-on-the-floor" riffs that are guaranteed to get your feet moving. Whereas the sixteenth note dominates the funk figures, the eighth note dominates here. As with the funk figures, timing is absolutely crucial to making these groove.

This figure features almost exclusively bass notes and *serious* syncopation. You may have to count through this one a few times in order to "feel" the riff properly. The grace notes in measure 2 (beat 3) and measure 4 (beat 2) provide a subtle touch that keeps the riff from sounding stale.

21 Fig. 21

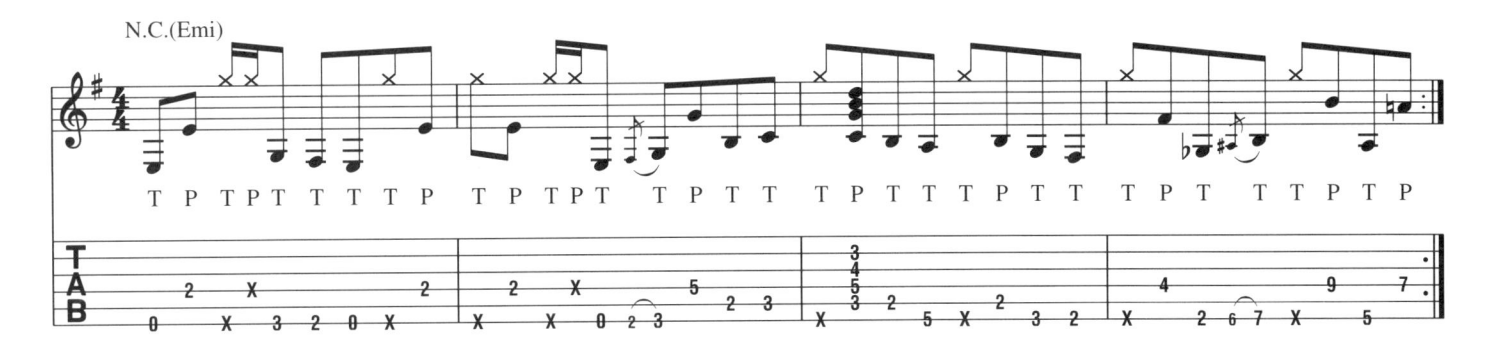

Chord punches and walking bass lines dominate in figures 22 and 23. Notice again in fig. 22 that the progression repeats exactly with the exception of the last chord; this concept can also be found in fig. 19.

22 Fig. 22

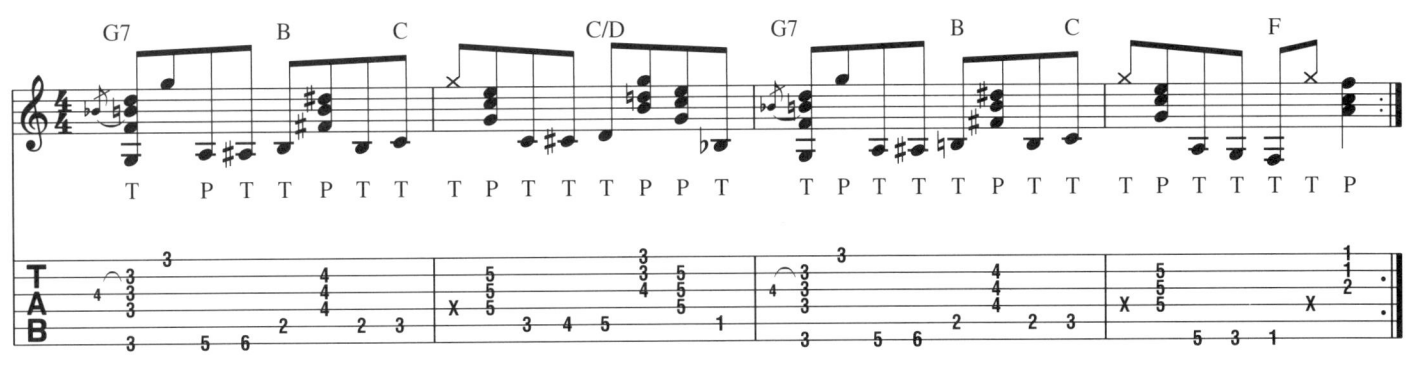

23 Fig. 23

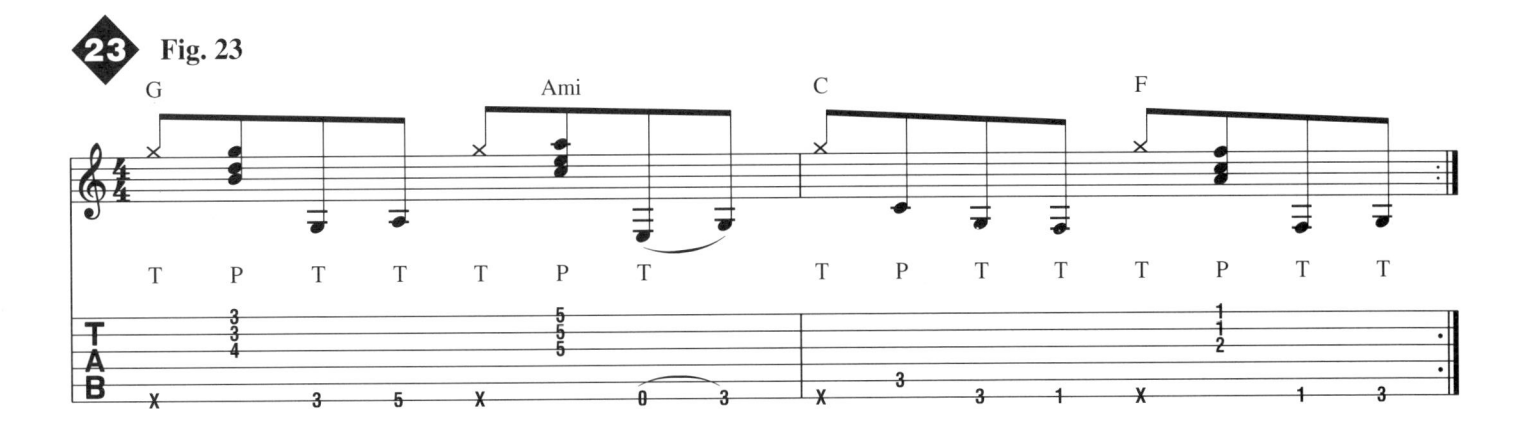

13

Syncopation once again drives fig. 24. Notice how the second, third, and fourth chords are all anticipated by one eighth note.

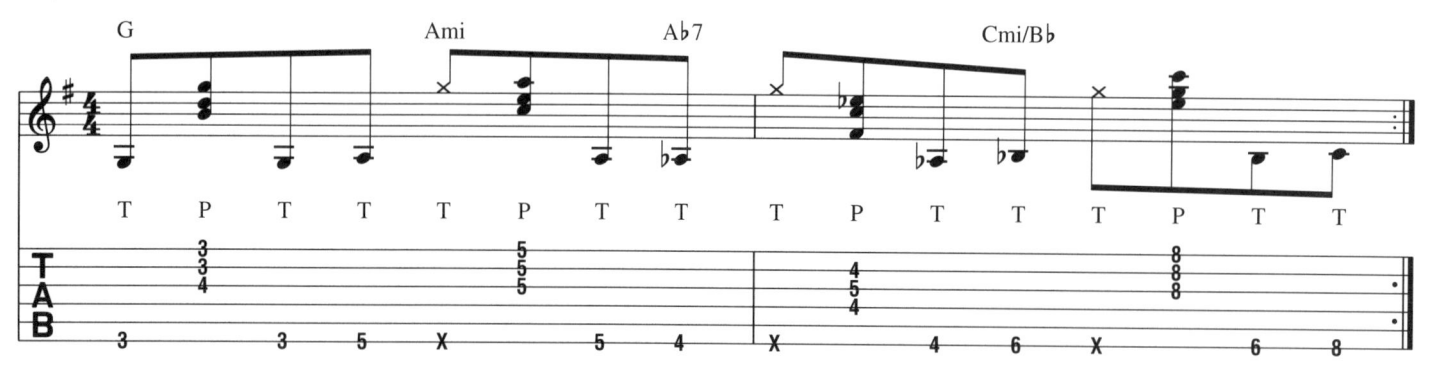

Fig. 24

In fig. 25, we see the slap technique applied to the common i–♭VII–♭VI progression. The syncopation found in fig. 24 can be found here as well. Notice again the subtle touch provided by the grace note hammer-on.

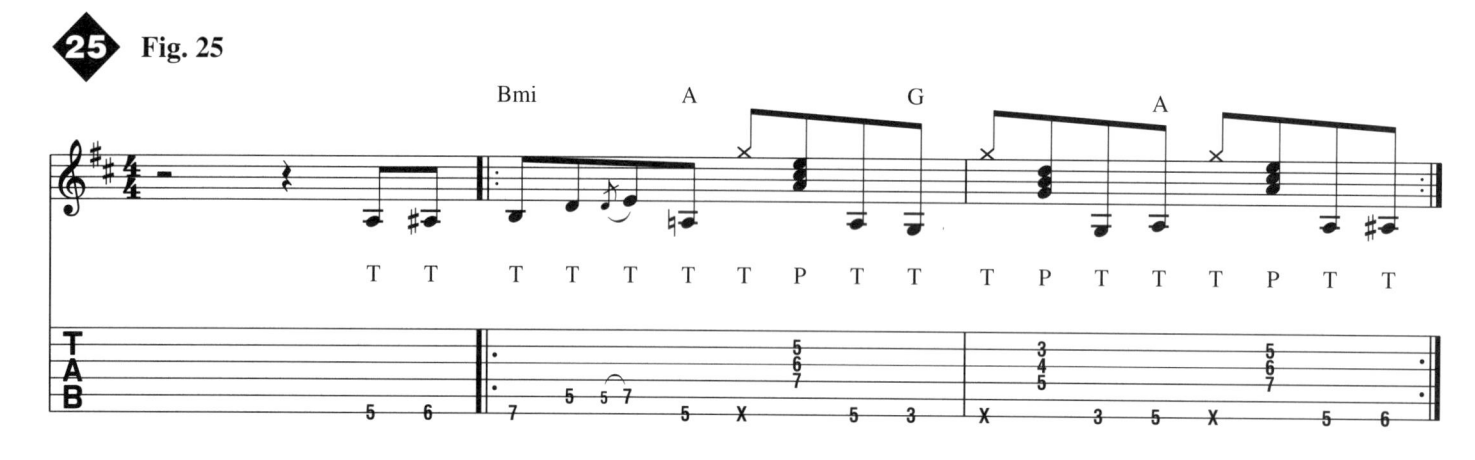

Fig. 25

This final funk-rock figure will be the only one that features a sixteenth-note feel. It's basically a vamp between Emi and C with a Phrygian-sounding F5 wrapping it up.

Fig. 26

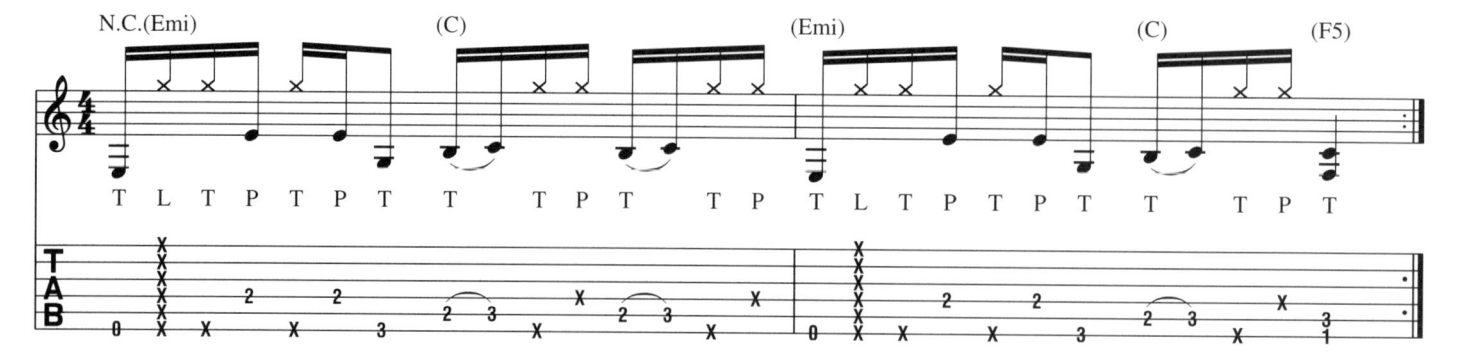

Chapter 3

R&B and Motown Figures

These figures provide a new perspective and outlook on these guitar-dominated genres.

The following two figures feature syncopated chord punches and compound meter.

Fig. 27

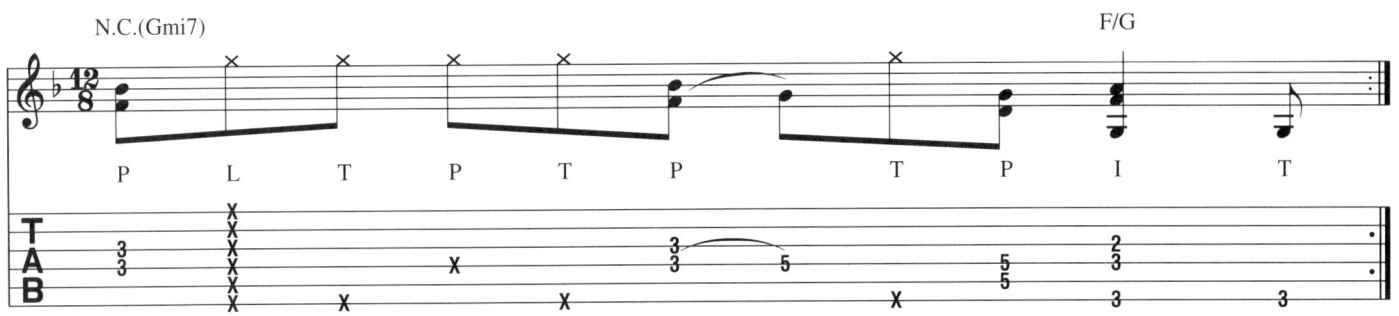

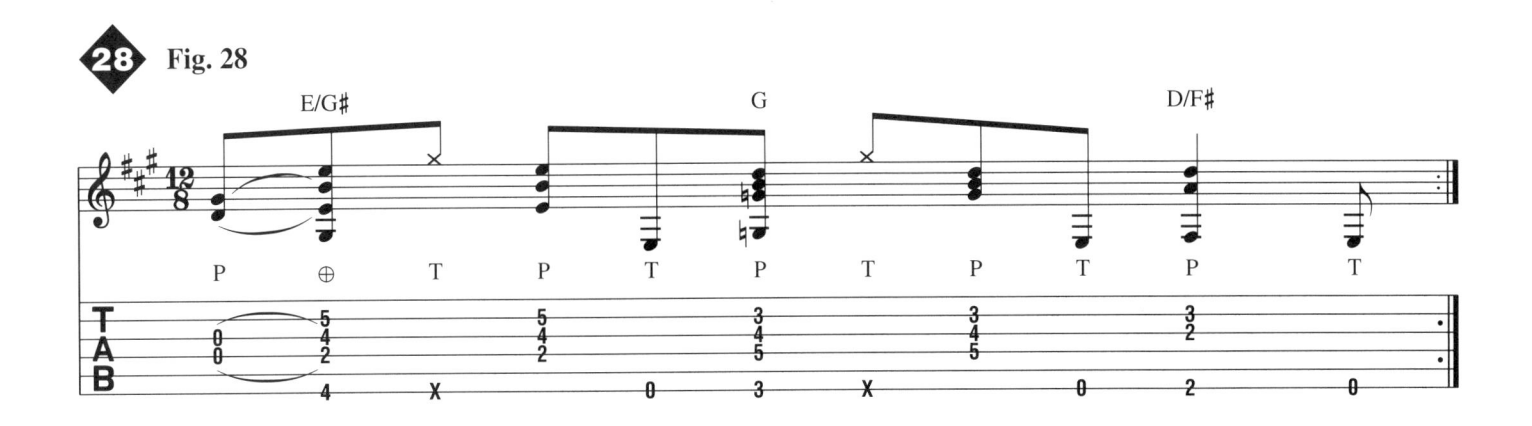

Fig. 28

Figure 29 planes dominant 7th chords with a syncopated feel. Notice the percussive left-hand slap in measure 2 (beat 2), providing variety to the otherwise repeated pattern.

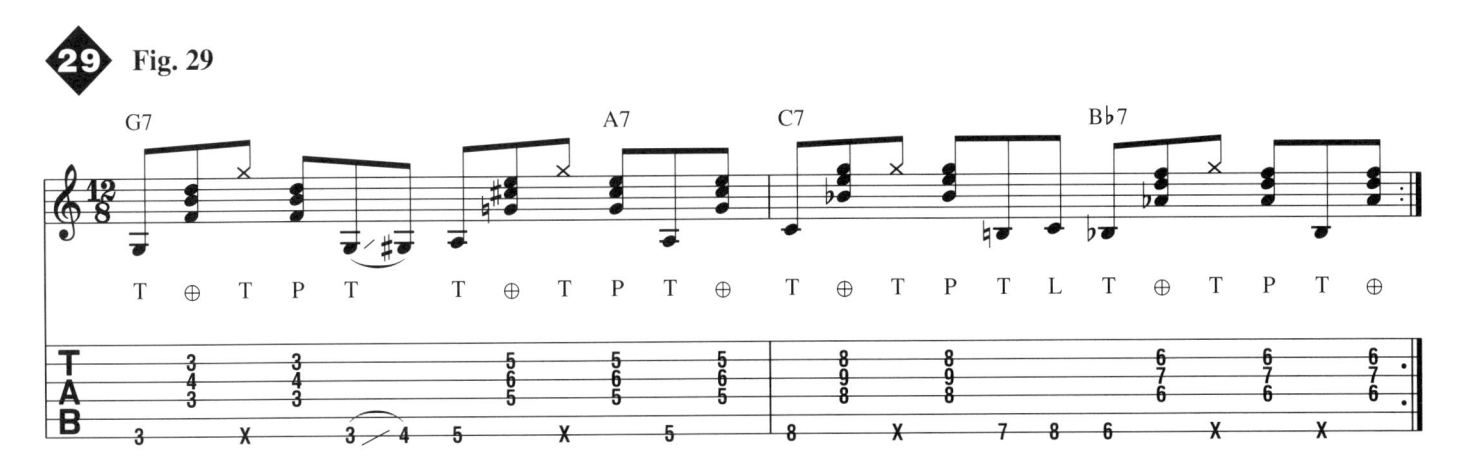

Fig. 29

This next figure combines a typical Motown progression (I–IV–V–vi) with a smooth funk feel. Notice the first-inversion I chord and the bright Ama7 sounds in the first and third measures.

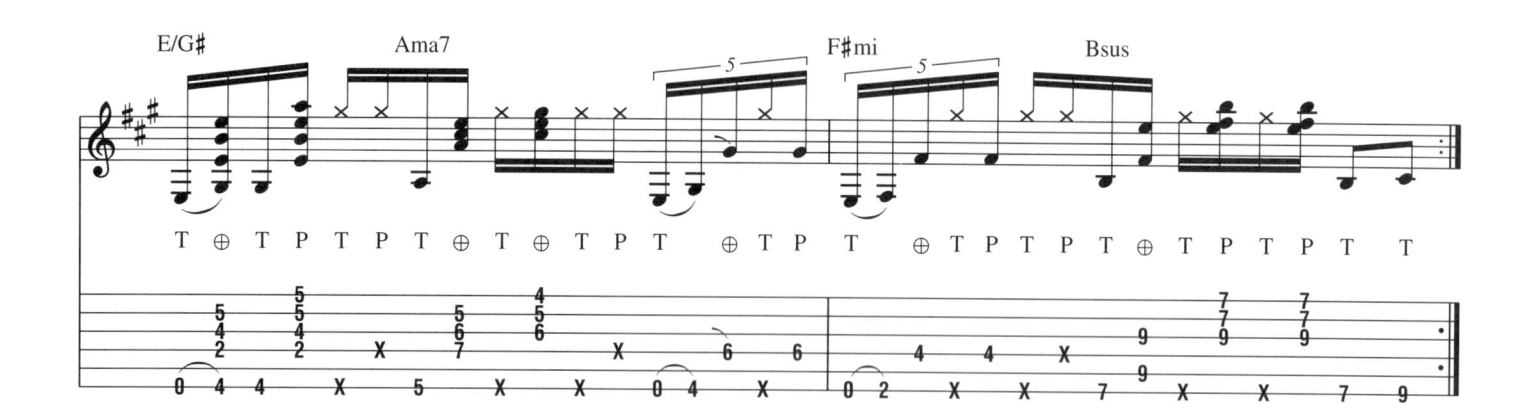

Fig. 30

Chapter 4

Latin and Reggae Figures

The following riffs provide yet another application of this technique for guitar. The key to many of these figures is the separation of the bass and treble. Both of these genres usually feature chordal accompaniment that is both sparse and exact. With attention to detail, it is possible to effectively simulate both roles (bass and accompaniment) with one guitar part.

This Latin figure is built on a repeating bass figure. It features a very common progression.

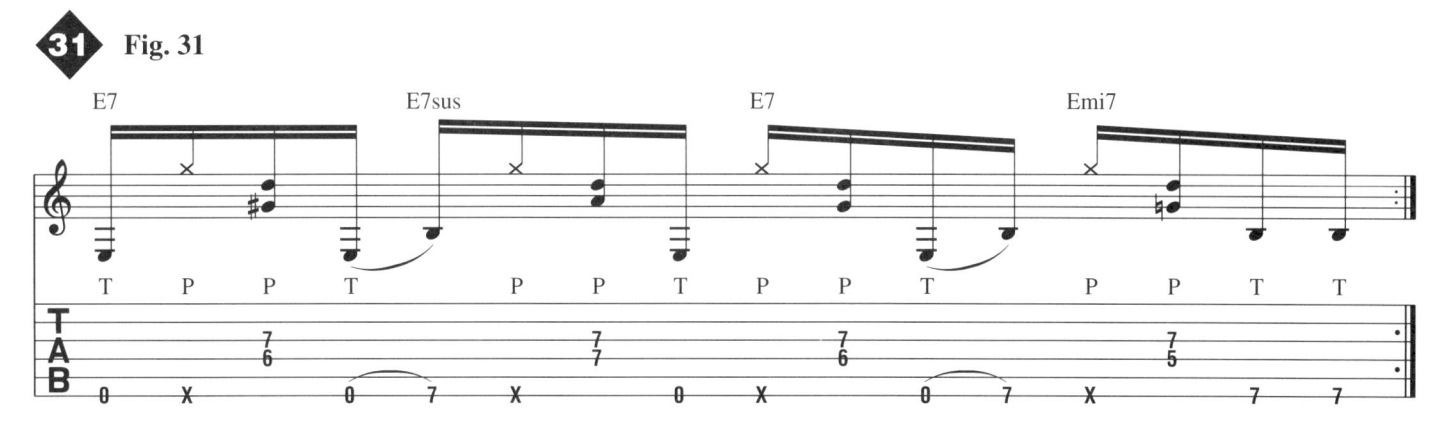

Fig. 31

Watch for the syncopated chords in figure 32. Notice also the use of the open low E string in the bass figure. Figure 33 sequences a I–IV progression up a whole step. Notice the chromatic walking bass figure on beat 4 of each measure. Figure 34 demonstrates a single-guitar approach to imitating a reggae feel.

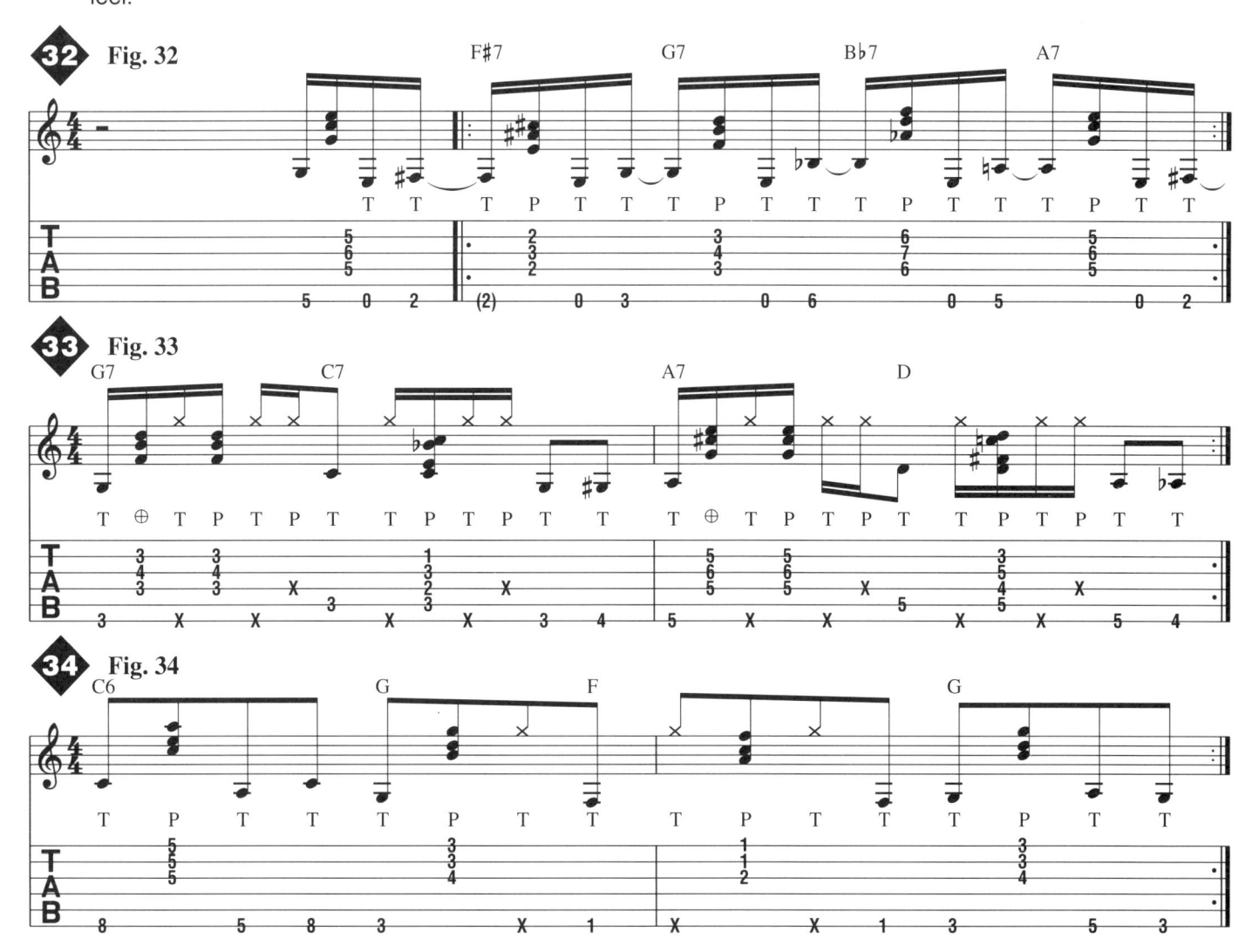

Fig. 32

Fig. 33

Fig. 34

Chapter 5

Technical Exercises

This chapter will provide several figures that concentrate on one or two specific techniques each. They'll allow you to work on the skills needed for the rest of this book in a somewhat musical context.

The following two exercises nail home the left-hand hammer-on technique. The harmony in figure 35 consists of quartal sonorities (chords built upon stacked 4ths).

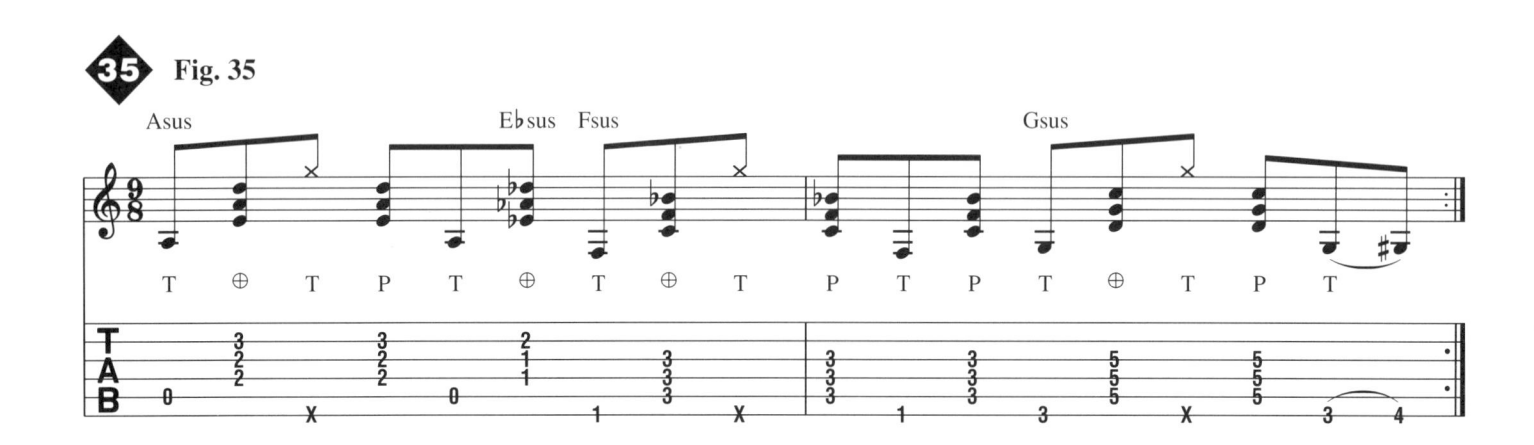

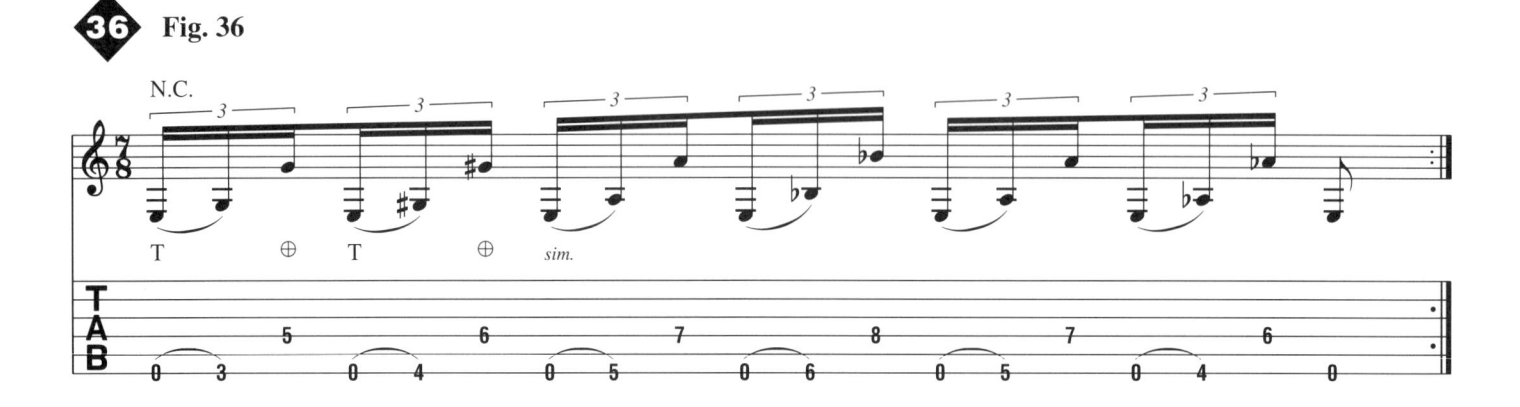

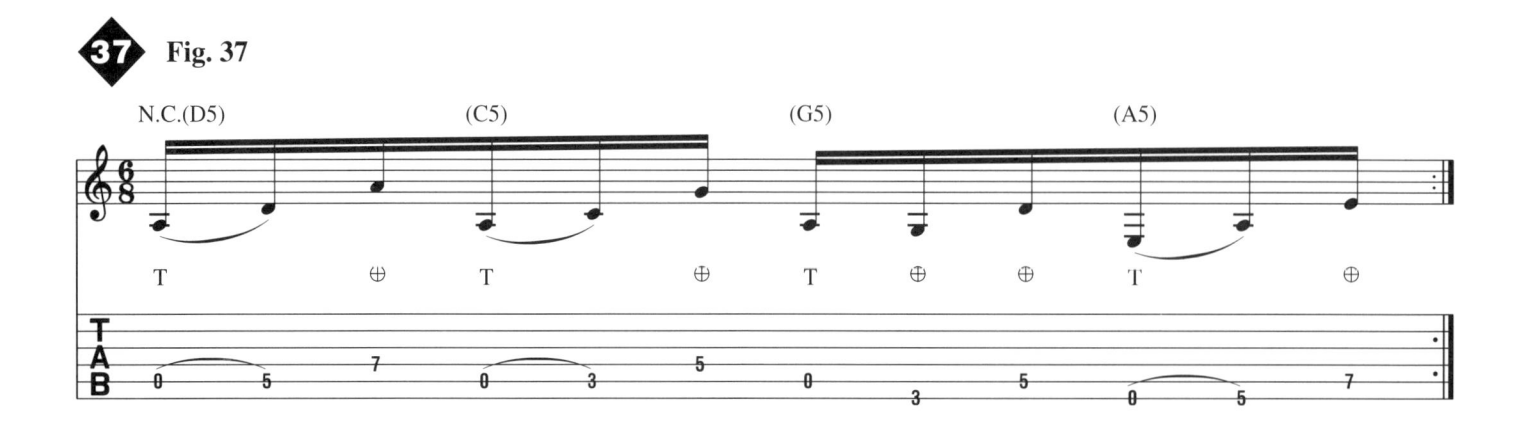

Fig. 35

Fig. 36

Fig. 37

These next figures concentrate on both left-hand hammer-ons and right-hand tapping.

Fig. 38

Fig. 39

This figure requires precise slapping of open strings as well as precise hammer-ons.

Fig. 40

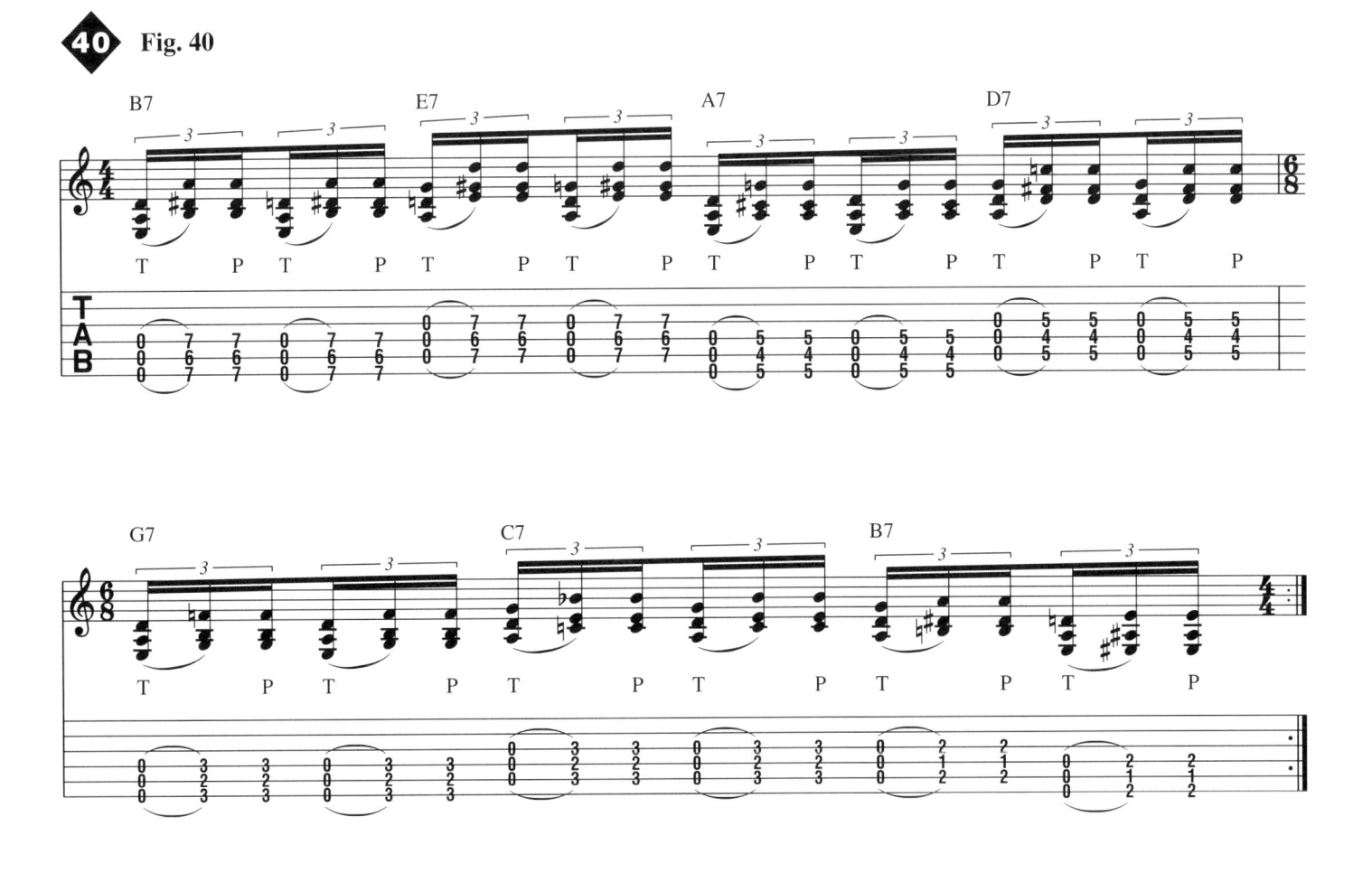

The following two figures combine slapping, left-hand hammer-ons, and popping.

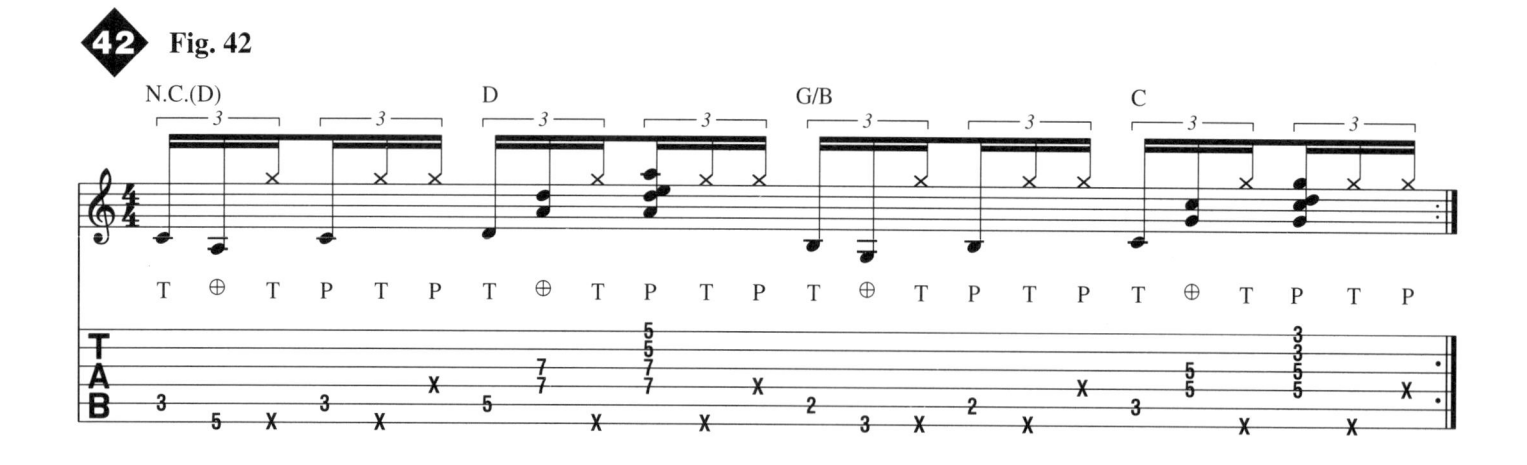

These remaining figures concentrate strictly on percussive exercises. This is a great way to work on timing. Since the rhythmic ticks are the only thing heard, it's very easy to hear if you're rushing or dragging a bit.

Fig. 43

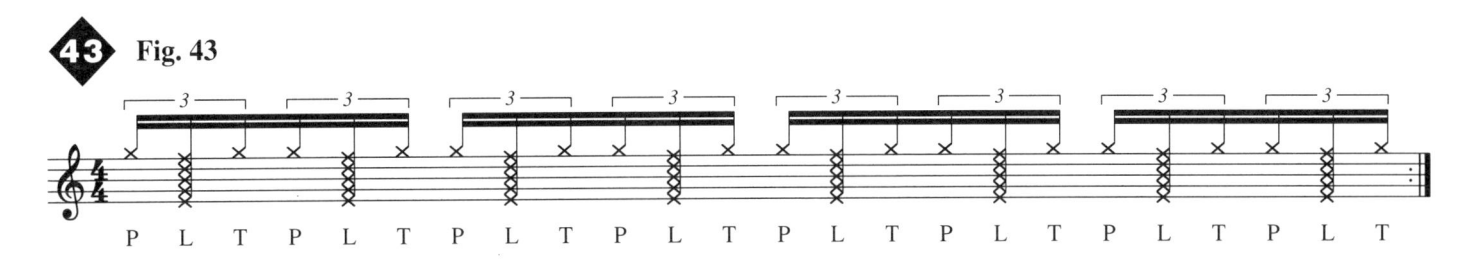

P L T P L T P L T P L T P L T P L T P L T P L T

Fig. 44

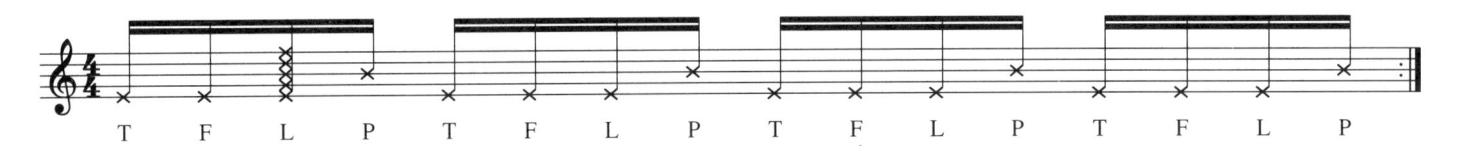

T F L P T F L P T F L P T F L P

Fig. 45

T L T P T L T P T L T P T L T P

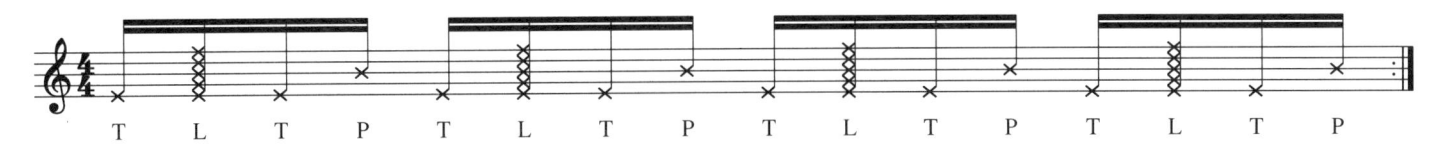

For these latin percussion exercises, mute the strings with your left hand. The thumb notes here are normal thumb strokes (not slaps).

Fig. 46

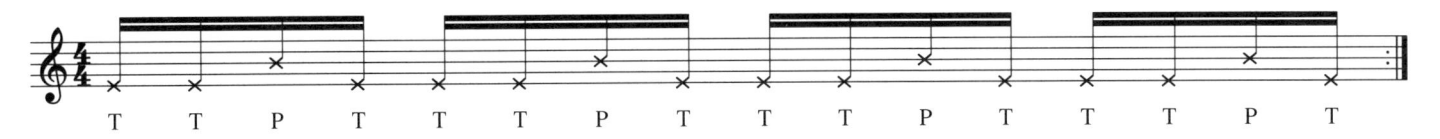

T T P T T T P T T T P T T T P T

Fig. 47

T T P T T T P T T T P T T T P T

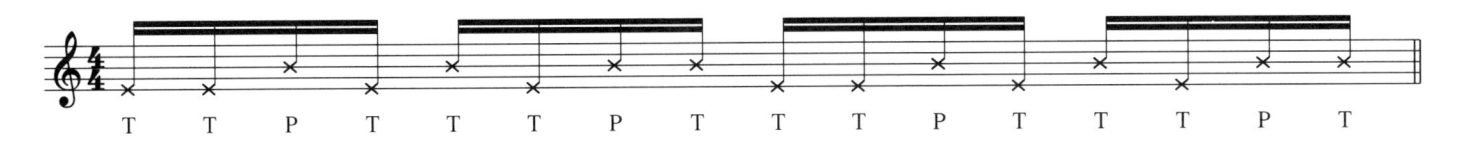

These two figures concentrate strictly on slaps and pops.

Fig. 48

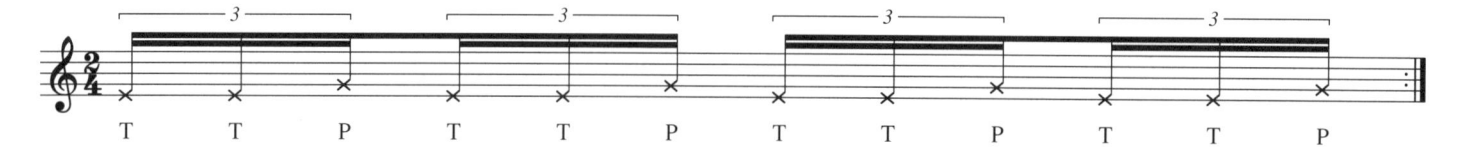

T T P T T P T T P T T P

Fig. 49

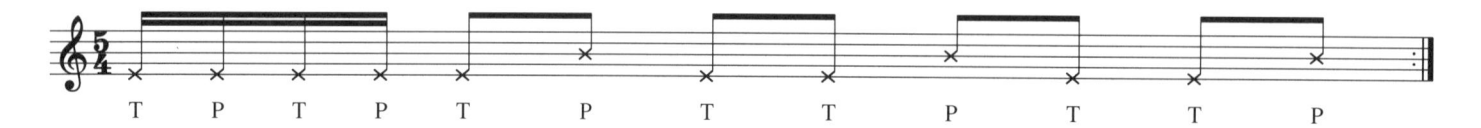

T P T P T P T T P T T P

The remaining few figures combine slaps, pops, and left-hand hammer-ons with a straight sixteenth-note feel. Notice the syncopated accents.

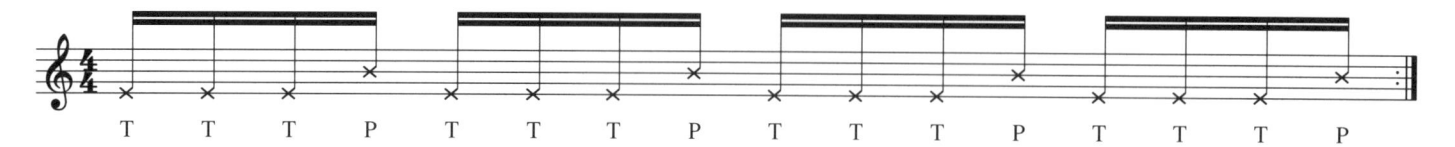

Fig. 50

T T T P T T T P T T T P T T T P

Fig. 51

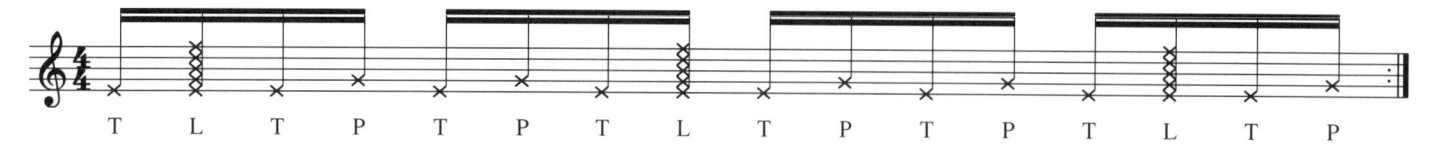

T L T P T P T L T P T P T L T P

Fig. 52

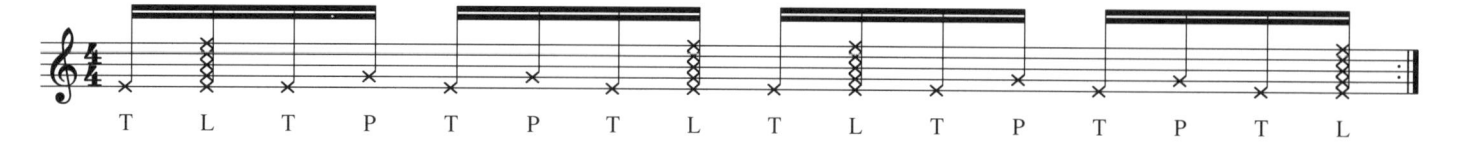

T L T P T P T L T L T P T P T L

Acknowledgments

I would like to thank Jonathan Merkel for transcribing, editing, and preparing the musical examples in this book, as well as engineering and recording the audio CD.

Thank you: Jessie Kreger for your assistance, Nick Roubas for your guitar, and all at Hal Leonard Corporation.

Special thanks go to Marie-Christine Belkadi for maintaining my website:
www.home.earthlink.net/~mcb1
email: mcb1@earthlink.net

This book is dedicated to Ted Greene—my favorite chord melody player in the world.

About the Author

Jean-Marc Belkadi started playing guitar at age 14. He graduated from the Toulouse Music Conservatory in his hometown. In 1984, he left France for the U.S. to study at Musicians Institute in Los Angeles where he received the Best Guitarist of the Year award.

In 1989 and 1992, he was awarded third and second prize at the Billboard Song Contest. For three years, he was musical director of the Johnny Hune TV show. He has written three guitar method books—*A Modern Approach to Jazz, Rock, and Fusion Guitar*, *The Diminished Scale for Guitar*, and *Advanced Scale Concepts and Licks for Guitar*—and has recorded one solo album.

Musicians Institute Press

is the official series of Southern California's renowned music school, Musicians Institute. **MI** instructors, some of the finest musicians in the world, share their vast knowledge and experience with you – no matter what your current level. For guitar, bass, drums, vocals, and keyboards, **MI Press** offers the finest music curriculum for higher learning through a variety of series:

ESSENTIAL CONCEPTS
Designed from MI core curriculum programs.

MASTER CLASS
Designed from MI elective courses.

PRIVATE LESSONS
Tackle a variety of topics "one-on-one" with MI faculty instructors.

BASS

Arpeggios for Bass
by Dave Keif • Private Lessons
00695133 .... $12.95

The Art of Walking Bass
A Method for Acoustic or Electric Bass
by Bob Magnusson • Master Class
00695168 Book/CD Pack $17.95

Bass Fretboard Basics
by Paul Farnen • Essential Concepts
00695201 .... $12.95

Bass Playing Techniques
by Alexis Sklarevski • Essential Concepts
00695207 .... $16.95

Grooves for Electric Bass
by David Keif • Private Lessons
00695265 Book/CD Pack $14.95

Latin Bass
The Essential Guide to Afro-Cuban and Brazilian Styles
by George Lopez and David Keif • Private Lessons
00695543 Book/CD Pack $14.95

Music Reading for Bass
by Wendy Wrehovcsik • Essential Concepts
00695203 .... $9.95

Odd-Meter Bassics
by Dino Monoxelos • Private Lessons
00695170 Book/CD Pack $14.95

GUITAR

Advanced Scale Concepts & Licks for Guitar
by Jean Marc Belkadi • Private Lessons
00695298 Book/CD Pack $14.95

Basic Blues Guitar
by Steve Trovato • Private Lessons
00695180 Book/CD Pack $12.95

Contemporary Acoustic Guitar
by Eric Paschal & Steve Trovato • Master Class
00695320 Book/CD Pack $14.95

Classical & Fingerstyle Guitar Techniques
by David Oakes • Master Class
00695171 Book/CD Pack $14.95

Creative Chord Shapes
by Jamie Findlay • Private Lessons
00695172 Book/CD Pack $9.95

Diminished Scale for Guitar
by Jean Marc Belkadi • Private Lessons
00695227 Book/CD Pack $9.95

Essential Rhythm Guitar
Patterns, Progressions and Techniques for All Styles
by Steve Trovato • Private Lessons
00695181 Book/CD Pack $14.95

Funk Guitar: The Essential Guide
by Ross Bolton • Private Lessons
00695419 Book/CD Pack $9.95

Guitar Basics
by Bruce Buckingham • Private Lessons
00695134 Book/CD Pack $14.95

Guitar Hanon
by Peter Deneff • Private Lessons
00695321 .... $9.95

Guitar Soloing
by Dan Gilbert & Beth Marlis • Essential Concepts
00695190 Book/CD Pack $19.95

Harmonics for Guitar
by Jamie Findlay • Private Lessons
00695169 Book/CD Pack $9.95

Jazz Guitar Chord System
by Scott Henderson • Private Lessons
00695291 .... $6.95

Jazz Guitar Improvisation
by Sid Jacobs • Master Class
00695128 Book/CD Pack $17.95

Jazz-Rock Triad Improvising
by Jean Marc Belkadi • Private Lessons
00695361 Book/CD Pack $12.95

Latin Guitar
The Essential Guide to Brazilian and Afro-Cuban Rhythms
by Bruce Buckingham • Master Class
00695379 Book/CD Pack $14.95

Modern Approach to Jazz, Rock & Fusion Guitar
by Jean Marc Belkadi • Private Lessons
00695143 Book/CD Pack $14.95

Modes for Guitar
by Tom Kolb • Private Lessons
00695555 Book/CD Pack $16.95

Music Reading for Guitar
by David Oakes • Essential Concepts
00695192 .... $16.95

The Musician's Guide to Recording Acoustic Guitar
by Dallan Beck • Private Lessons
00695505 Book/CD Pack $12.95

Practice Trax for Guitar
by Danny Gill • Private Lessons
00695601 Book/CD Pack $14.95

Rhythm Guitar
by Bruce Buckingham & Eric Paschal • Essential Concepts
00695188 .... $16.95

Rock Lead Basics
by Nick Nolan & Danny Gill • Master Class
00695144 Book/CD Pack $14.95

Rock Lead Performance
by Nick Nolan & Danny Gill • Master Class
00695278 Book/CD Pack $16.95

Rock Lead Techniques
by Nick Nolan & Danny Gill • Master Class
00695146 Book/CD Pack $14.95

Texas Blues Guitar
by Robert Calva • Private Lessons
00695340 Book/CD Pack $14.95

KEYBOARD

Funk Keyboards – The Complete Method
A Contemporary Guide to Chords, Rhythms, and Licks
by Gail Johnson • Master Class
00695336 Book/CD Pack $14.95

Jazz Hanon
by Peter Deneff • Private Lessons
00695554 .... $12.95

Keyboard Technique
by Steve Weingard • Essential Concepts
00695365 .... $12.95

Keyboard Voicings: The Complete Guide
by Kevin King • Essential Concepts
00695209 .... $12.95

Music Reading for Keyboard
by Larry Steelman • Essential Concepts
00695205 .... $12.95

R&B Soul Keyboards
by Henry J. Brewer • Private Lessons
00695327 Book/CD Pack $16.95

Salsa Hanon
by Peter Deneff • Private Lessons
00695226 .... $10.95

DRUM

Afro-Cuban Coordination for Drumset
by Maria Martinez • Private Lessons
00695328 Book/CD Pack $14.95

Brazilian Coordination for Drumset
by Maria Martinez • Master Class
00695284 Book/CD Pack $14.95

Chart Reading Workbook for Drummers
by Bobby Gabriele • Private Lessons
00695129 Book/CD Pack $14.95

Drummer's Guide to Odd Meters
by Ed Roscehi • Essential Concepts
00695349 Book/CD Pack $14.95

Latin Soloing for Drumset
by Phil Maturano • Private Lessons
00695287 Book/CD Pack $14.95

Working the Inner Clock for Drumset
by Phil Maturano • Private Lessons
00695127 Book/CD Pack $16.95

VOICE

Harmony Vocals: The Essential Guide
by Mike Campbell & Tracee Lewis • Private Lessons
00695262 Book/CD Pack $16.95

Sightsinging
by Mike Campbell • Essential Concepts
00695195 .... $16.95

ALL INSTRUMENTS

An Approach to Jazz Improvisation
by Dave Pozzi • Private Lessons
00695135 Book/CD Pack $17.95

Encyclopedia of Reading Rhythms
by Gary Hess • Private Lessons
00695145 .... $19.95

Going Pro
by Kenny Kerner • Private Lessons
00695322 .... $16.95

Harmony & Theory
by Keith Wyatt & Carl Schroeder • Essential Concepts
00695161 .... $17.95

Lead Sheet Bible
by Robin Randall • Private Lessons
00695130 Book/CD Pack $19.95

WORKSHOP SERIES
Transcribed scores of the greatest songs ever!

Blues Workshop
00695137 .... $22.95

Classic Rock Workshop
00695136 .... $19.95

FOR MORE INFORMATION, SEE YOUR LOCAL MUSIC DEALER, OR WRITE TO:

HAL•LEONARD® CORPORATION
7777 W. BLUEMOUND RD. P.O. BOX 13819 MILWAUKEE, WI 53213

Visit Hal Leonard Online at
www.halleonard.com

Prices, contents, and availability subject to change without notice. Some products may not be available outside of the U.S.A.

0801